OPERATING IN THE CHAOS

A Black Woman's Guide to Managing External and Internal Chaos

Michelle Boone-Thornton, EdD, QMHP
Debbie Hood, PhD, LPC, ACS
Marcia Stewart, EdD

Published by Weird Disciple Publishing

Edited by Marrisa Thornton, Articulate

ISBN #978-1-966979-06-7

TABLE OF CONTENTS

Foreword

Navigating the Storm—When the Outside World Comes In

There is "**A CHAOS**" that lives inside us - our doubts, our weariness, our fears. But there is another chaos. A louder one. The kind that lives outside of us, in boardrooms, classrooms, break-rooms, and invisible systems. It's the chaos of doing more than everyone else and being rewarded with silence.

Of being qualified but questioned. Present but unseen. Necessary but unpaid. Of carrying the burden and the blame - without the title, the voice, or the seat at the table.

The chapter, **External Chaos**, is for the women who show up every day in environments that were not built for their brilliance, but who keep showing up anyway. It is for the woman who knows what it means to be the storm-stopper, the peacekeeper, the fixer, the face of professionalism, and still feels invisible in the process.

The external environment we navigate is more than background noise. It's the system. The unspoken. The storm. And learning how to see it clearly, name it truthfully, and respond to it strategically is more than healing - it's survival.

It's justice. It's leadership.

The chapter, **Internal Chaos**, we are not blaming ourselves for what we inherited. We are examining the winds - the tornado of over-functioning, the typhoon of over-qualification, the floods of burnout, the hurricanes of exclusion, the earthquakes of imbalance, the sinkholes of identity loss - and we are saying:

"This is not mine to carry anymore."

This work is personal - but it's also structural.

This is not just a tool for reflection.

This is a framework for liberation - one that challenges women to unlearn the roles we were assigned and reclaim the leadership we were born into.

If we want equity in the workplace, we must first be willing to see the systems that create inequity.

If we want to change the climate, we must stop normalizing storms.

The chapter, **Managing External and Internal Chaos**, is your forecast.

It will teach you how to protect your peace, elevate your worth, draw bold boundaries, and stop shrinking in environments that are too small for your power.

You are not here to carry the chaos. You are here to shift it.

Let the **JOURNEY** of managing the chaos external and internal to our state of being **BEGIN**!!!!

About the Authors

Dr. Michelle Boone-Thornton, Ed.D., QMHP, is a nationally recognized educator, mental health strategist, author, speaker, and advocate for women's empowerment and workplace equity.

Known affectionately as "The Unmasking Guru," she is the author of Transforming Your Reality: Removing the Mask and the forthcoming *Lessons from the Mourners Bench: A Bench, A Bible, and a Praying Auntie*, which explores generational healing through faith, reflection, and truth-telling.

As a World Civility Ambassador, Dr. Boone-Thornton's inter-national work aligns with her stateside mission—to equip underserved communities with the tools, language, and frameworks necessary to restore emotional wellness, navigate generational trauma, and cultivate transformative leadership rooted in compassion, faith, and justice. Her global presence reflects a consistent commitment to inclusion, dignity, and culturally responsive healing wherever she serves.

Debbie Hood, PhD, LPC, ACS, is the owner/ CEO of S.E.E. Clinical Services, LLC. Dr. Debbie Hood is committed to Strengthening, Educating, and Empowering women, children, families, and communities. Dr. Hood also provides training and clinical supervision for novice counselors.

Dr. Hood received her B.S. in Psychology from Francis Marion University (South Carolina) and an M.S. in Rehabilitation Counseling from Virginia Commonwealth University, before eventually earning a Doctor of Philosophy – Counselor Education and Supervision from Regent University (2011). Dr. Hood has had an extensive history of working in children's mental health services. From an early start working in a daycare, group home setting, and inpatient psychiatric residential treatment center, she has been dedicated to becoming a holistic provider of mental health services.

Marcia Stewart, Ed.D., is a retired Navy Veteran, an international speaker, an international author, and a Coach who uses her experience and knowledge in workforce development to build and grow the workforce and leaders of tomorrow.

Dr. Stewart uses her certifications in Coaching and Gallup to collaborate with organizations and individuals to identify ways to grow engagement, leaders, and employees and improve day-to-day operations.

She continuously gives back to the community through her volunteer efforts with DAV, NABVETS, OSHAMA, HRISPI, and mentoring with in-person and virtual middle and high school students.

Workbook Introduction

In today's fast-paced world, the workplace can often feel like a relentless storm, tossing us from one demand to the next with little chance to catch our breath. We juggle endless responsibilities, navigate shifting expectations, and strive to make our efforts visible in an environment that often values output over well-being. Amid this turbulence, it's easy to lose sight of our worth and become overwhelmed by forces beyond our control.

This book is your guide through the chaos—an invitation to pause, reflect, and reclaim your narrative. Drawing on real-world experiences and insightful activities, each chapter illuminates a unique storm we face on the job, from being overqualified yet undervalued, to shouldering invisible workloads without recognition or support. You'll find practical tools designed to help you identify where your energy is being spent, assess what is truly yours to carry, and chart a new course toward balance and self-advocacy.

Whether you're feeling lost in the whirlwind of multitasking, shut out from decision-making, or burdened by unreasonable expect-ations, this book offers validation, strategies, and a sense of solid-arity. It empowers you not only to weather the storms, but to emerge stronger—with clarity, confidence, and a renewed sense of purpose.

Let's embark on this journey together and transform chaos into an opportunity for growth, resilience, and meaningful change.

Chapter 1

External Chaos

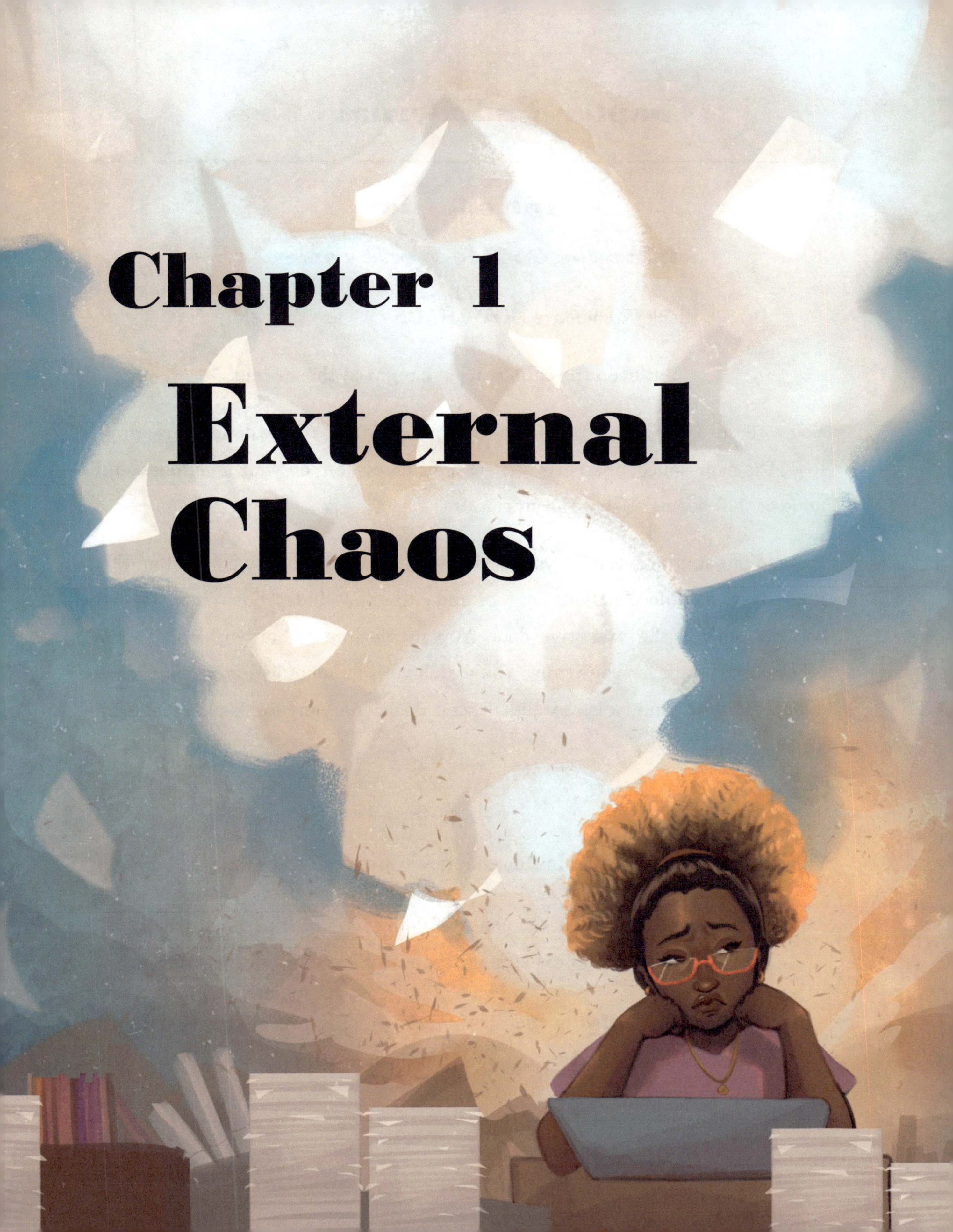

Chapter 1 – External Chaos

Introduction

When the Outside World Comes In

Black Women are **NOT CHAOS** - we are the calm.

But even the calm can get caught in the storm.

You walk into work prepared. Polished. Credentialed. You've done the reading, lived the experience, and carry generations of wisdom on your shoulders. But none of that seems to stop the storm.

Instead of being honored for your strength, you're expected to do it all and fix it all—with a smile. You earn degrees and gather accolades, but you're still left waiting outside the executive door. You juggle impossible workloads while others take credit for your calm. You watch your value questioned, your ideas dismissed, and your voice excluded from decisions you're asked to clean up after.

You are not imagining it.

This storm has names. And in this chapter, we will call them out:

- ***Tornado Warning*** is the chaos of doing too much and being seen too little. It's the exhausting spin of responsibility with-out recognition.
- ***Typhoon of Titles*** is the dissonance of being overqualified and still undervalued—collecting degrees that open no doors.

- ***Flooded and Forgotten*** speaks to the burnout of carrying teams, emotions, and expectations with no life raft in sight.
- ***Hurricane Boardroom*** is the exclusion from leadership, even as you stabilize what others disrupt.
- ***Earthquake of Expectations*** is being asked to hold up shaky systems and clean up messes you didn't create.
- ***Sinkhole of Self-Worth*** is the erosion of identity when chaos is normalized and your peace becomes a sacrifice.

But here is the truth:

You are **NOT** the problem. The systems, structures, and cultures that *pretend not to see you* - they are. And this chapter is about reclaiming your voice, power, and peace, even in the eye of external storms.

"The Lord will fight for you; you need only to be still." — Exodus 14:14 (NIV)

Here, you will name the storm. Then you will speak life into yourself.

You will draw boundaries, cast vision, and walk away from what was never yours to carry.

The world may be in chaos—but you?

You are operating in clarity.

Tornado Warning: Doing Too Much While Being Seen Too Little

She's everywhere. Fixing everything. But no one sees her.

You might as well be the invisible woman! A tornado doesn't announce its arrival - it builds quietly, then rips through everything. For many black women in the workplace, the tornado becomes a way of life. You are the first to respond, the last to leave, the one holding things together when everyone else is falling apart. You're praised as "strong," "resilient," and "reliable," but rarely as "leader," "visionary," or "deserving of rest."

And yet, you still show up.

"Come to me, all who are weary and burdened, and I will give you rest." — Matthew 11:28 (NIV)

But being the center of the storm takes a toll. Doing too much while being seen too little creates a dangerous cycle: the more competent you appear, the more is piled onto your plate—and the less likely others are to advocate for your elevation, your rest, or your recognition.

Black women are paid 64 cents for every dollar earned by White men and are promoted at significantly lower rates, despite often having higher levels of education and experience.

(Source: Lean In / McKinsey & Company, 2023 Women in the Workplace Report)

Activity 1: Tornado Siren

Do you know when the storm is brewing? Let's identify your *tornado siren*. The metaphorical siren, that will help you pause, name the storm, and redirect your energy from chaos to clarity. Use the Warning Signs Checklist below.

Check all that apply to you now or at any other time.

- I often work beyond my job description without acknowledgement
- I'm expected to fix problems I didn't create.
- I'm praised for being "strong" but not promoted.
- I feel guilty when I say no.
- I constantly pick up the slack for others.
- I show up early, stay late, and am still asked for more.
- I feel like I'm spinning but not moving forward.

Add your own if needed.

- ____
- ____
- ____
- ____

Activity 2: Reflection Prompt

Take a moment to sit with this question. Be truthful and honest. Drop the persona (mask of public identity) of "I'm here to help, let me show you, I'll get it for you, let me do it, what do you need......"

What part of the tornado am I in—and what would happen if I stepped out of it?

Write your response here:

Activity 3: Map the Chaos

1. Draw a tornado in the space below or imagine one in your mind.
2. In the center (the eye), write what *you* most value at work (e.g., peace, purpose, fairness, creativity).
3. Around the tornado's swirl, write all the tasks, roles, expectations, and chaos you're caught in—especially the ones that do not align with your values or job description.
4. Circle the ones that need boundaries. Cross out the ones you can let go.

(Use this space or your own notebook to draw and reflect)

Activity 4: Releasing the Spin

I don't have to do everything. I don't have to be everything. Being seen starts with seeing yourself. If you don't see you, no one else will either. Be seen my QUEEN!

List 3 ways you will slow the spin this week:

1. ______________________________

____

2. ______________________________

____

3. ______________________________

____

If you need additional space, here you go...

Activity 5: Affirmation

What you say to yourself is important; your words will refresh your brain, body, and soul. Say it!

Read it!

I will not shrink in the storm.

I will no longer confuse being busy with being valued.

I release the need to prove my worth through exhaustion.

I am seen, even when I rest.

Write It!

____

____

____

____

Write It!

____

____

____

____

Write It!

____

____

____

____

Typhoon of Titles: Overqualified, Undervalued

I collected degrees like armor… but they still don't see me as qualified.

A typhoon gains power from the ocean's heat, swelling in strength until it reaches the shore with undeniable force. Black Women often navigate the workplace with a similar approach, driven by drive, excellence, and perseverance. We gather degrees, certificates, advanced training, and experience not just to be better, but to be seen.

And yet… the recognition rarely matches the effort.

You were told education was the key. That excellence would open doors. But instead, you face job listings asking for less than what you bring, interviews that dismiss you, and pay scales that disrespect your credentials. Your brilliance is confined to roles far beneath your capabilities, while others with less are elevated ahead of you.

You are not alone—and you are not imagining it.

"For the Lord gives wisdom; from His mouth come knowledge and understanding." — Proverbs 2:6 (ESV)

The Credentials Crash

Black women are the most educated demographic by degree attainment among women in the U.S., yet they are underrepresented in senior leadership and earn significantly less across nearly all industries.

(Source: National Center for Education Statistics & American Association of University Women)

Activity 1: Reflection Prompt

"What was I told my education would provide? What has it actually brought me?"

Write your reflection here:

Activity 2: Reclaim the Power of Your Path

"Your journey is not just a résumé. It's a record of resilience."

You've worked hard. You've studied long. You've sacrificed sleep, finances, time with your family—and at times, your own well-being—all in pursuit of advancement, access, and respect. But if you're reading this, you may be realizing something painful:

You did everything "right," and the system still made you feel invisible.

This activity is not here to rehash your frustration. It's here to help you reclaim the meaning, purpose, and power behind your path—on your terms. Because your degrees, training, certifications, and lived experience are not just bullet points on a CV, they are a comprehensive representation of your qualifications. They are weapons, wisdom, and worth.

Let's shift the narrative.

Instructions:

1. Look at the chart on the next pages. You'll see three columns:

    - What I've Earned
    - What It Cost Me
    - What I Deserve

2. In the first column, list out the degrees, certifications, licenses, or experiences you've acquired—formal and informal. Include what you've mastered through work, self-study, or lived experience. (*Don't hold back.*)
3. In the second column, reflect on the real costs of earning those things. Think about what you sacrificed—financially, emotionally, relationally, or spiritually.
4. In the third column, claim what you deserve based on what you've earned—not just in pay, but in visibility, opportunity, authority, and alignment. (*Be bold. Be honest. Be unapologetic.*)
5. Once you complete the chart, circle three things in the "What I Deserve" column. These will become your focus in the months ahead—what you will seek, ask for, or affirm within yourself.

What I've Earned	What It Cost Me	What I Deserve
Degree(s), Certifications	Time, sleep, money, and family sacrifice	Recognition, respect, and fair pay
Experience, Life Lessons	Burnout, being overlooked	Leadership, trust, influence
Skills from unpaid labor	Emotional toll, invisibility	Career alignment, promotion

What I've Earned	What It Cost Me	What I Deserve

Activity 3: Deconstructing the Myth

Complete the following statements in your own words:

1. More education was supposed to bring me ________.
2. Instead, I often experience ________.
3. But from this point forward, I will redefine success as _________.

Use the space below to expand your statements.

Activity 4: Affirmation

What you say to yourself is important; your words will refresh your brain, body, and soul. Say it!

Read it!

"My value is not up for debate.
I am not overqualified—I am underutilized.
My credentials are not for decoration.
They are evidence of who I am and what I've overcome."

Write It!

____

____

____

____

Write It!

____

____

____

____

Write It!

____

____

____

Redirection: 3 Actions to Reclaim Your Power

1. I will stop shrinking my résumé to make others comfortable.
2. I will apply for the position I want, not just the one I'm "allowed."
3. I will track my wins—and use them to advocate for myself.

(*Write your own, if you'd like*)

4. ____
5. ____

Flooded and Forgotten: Drowning in Tasks with No Life Raft

"I'm doing everything, but no one seems to notice I'm barely staying afloat."

Floodwater rises gradually. At first, it's a small trickle—an extra assignment here, a project there. You say yes because you're capable. You keep going because others depend on you. But eventually, the water reaches your neck, and you're left treading water in silence, while others stand on dry ground—oblivious, or worse, indifferent.

For many Black Women in professional spaces, this flood looks like doing the work of two or three people, picking up others' slack, navigating emotional labor, and being the first to volunteer and the last to leave. You float between responsibilities without a lifeline—without support, credit, or relief.

"When you pass through the waters, I will be with you; and when you pass through the rivers, they will not sweep over you." — Isaiah 43:2 (NIV)

My sisters, this is your reminder: You were never meant to carry it all. You are allowed to rest. You are allowed to say, *"This is too much."* Your worth is not measured by how much you can endure.

Black women report the highest levels of burnout across all racial groups in the U.S. workforce. Many cite a lack of support, unequal workloads, and being perceived as "strong enough to handle anything" as contributors. (Source: Deloitte Women @ Work Global Survey, 2023)

Activity 1: Reflection Prompt

Take a moment to think about this, as it can be challenging to see yourself when you're busy carrying other people's burdens. You normalize it, personalize it, and add it to the many things you carry in your oversized purse - let's empty it out now!

"What tasks am I carrying that are not mine to carry?"
"What would support look like for me?"

Write your thoughts here:

___

___

___

___

___

___

___

___

___

___

___

___

Activity 2: Build Your Life Raft

In the midst of a flood, survival depends on having something to hold on to. Let's name the people, practices, and boundaries that can keep you afloat.

1. My Support – Who or what can I rely on?

   ____

   ____

   ____

2. My Boundaries – Where do I need to say "no"?

   ____

   ____

   ____

3. My Needs – What am I not getting at work?

   ____

   ____

   ____

Now, circle at least one thing from each column you will act on this week, the one thing you want to change…

Activity 3: Warning Signs That You're Drowning

Check any that feel familiar:

- I'm doing tasks outside of my job description.
- I am expected to "figure it out" without guidance or tools.
- I haven't taken a real break in weeks or months.
- I'm holding onto projects that should have been reassigned.
- I'm praised for being "so dependable," but never for leadership.
- (Other: ______________________________)
- (Other: ______________________________)
- (Other: ______________________________)
- (Other: ______________________________)

Activity 4: Rewriting the Story

Complete the sentences below:

1. I am not lazy for needing help. I am human

2. I no longer accept the lie that rest is weakness. I know that

3. I will protect my peace by

Activity 5: Affirmation

What you say to yourself is important; your words will refresh your brain, body, and soul. **Say it!**

Read it!

I am not here to prove how much I can take.
I am worthy of support.
My strength is not in surviving alone, but in knowing when to reach for the raft.

Write It!

____

____

____

____

Write It!

____

____

____

____

Write It!

____

____

____

____

Hurricane Boardroom: Shut Out at the Executive Table

"I've held the foundation together – yet I'm still not invited to the table I help stabilize."

Hurricanes are powerful, wide-reaching forces. They don't just touch one area—they shake everything. In the workplace, Black Women often *are* the stabilizing force—the ones holding the team together, tending to culture, maintaining order amid change. But when it's time to make decisions, shape vision, or sit at the table, the storm intensifies.

You're asked to lead in private but not in public. To implement—but not to ideate. To support—but not to shape.

Your absence from the boardroom is not because you lack credentials. It's because of deep-rooted systems of exclusion. You're left on the outside—watching others break what you've quietly fixed.

"Do you see someone skilled in their work? They will stand before kings; they will not stand before obscure people."
Proverbs 22:29 (NRSV)

This is not about ego. It's about equity.
It's about challenging the norm that everyone gets a voice—except you!

Black women hold less than 2% of executive-level positions in corporate America, despite being among the fastest-growing groups of entrepreneurs and highly educated professionals.
(Source: Catalyst, 2023 Women in Leadership Study)

EXECUTIVE
PRESENCE
BEGINS WITH
SELF-PERMISSION

Activity 1: Reflection Prompt:

"Where in my career have I been silenced, excluded, or dismissed—despite being qualified?"

Write your response here:

Activity 2: Build Your Own Executive Seat

1. On a blank page or in the space below, draw a chair that represents your rightful place at the table.

2. Label each leg of the chair with what you bring: e.g., *Strategy, Wisdom, Insight, Courage.*

3. On the backrest, write the vision you want to lead.

4. Reflect: *What's keeping me from sitting in this chair? And who told me I couldn't?* ____

____

____

____

____

____

____

____

____

____

____

____

Use this space below for designing your CHAIR.

Activity 3: The Closed-Door Questions

Check any that resonate with you. If these questions do not address your specific situation, write ones that do:

- I'm asked to implement ideas I was never invited to help create.
- I've had my contributions credited to someone else.
- I watch less-experienced colleagues be promoted past me.
- I'm left out of meetings that affect my work.
- I'm told I'm "intimidating" or "not a good fit for leadership."
- (Other: ______________________________)
- (Other: ______________________________)
- (Other: ______________________________)
- (Other: ______________________________)
- (Other: ______________________________)
- (Other: ______________________________)

Activity 4: Reframe the Narrative

Complete the following:

1. Leadership is not a title, it's how I show up. Moving forward I plan to show up ____

2. I don't need permission to lead. I need the room to do it fully. This is how I will create that room

3. From now on, I will

Activity 5: Affirmation

What you say to yourself is important; your words will refresh your brain, body, and soul. Say it!

Read it!

"I am not the help. I am the strategist.
I will no longer ask for a seat at a table built on exclusion.
I will bring my own blueprint—and build with those who see me."

Write It!

____

____

____

Write It!

____

____

____

Write It!

____

____

____

NOT
EVERYTHING
BROKEN
IS YOURS
TO FIX
BOUNDARY

Earthquake of Expectations: Fixing What You Didn't Break

"I'm expected to hold it all together... even when I didn't cause the cracks."

Earthquakes shake everything—foundations crack, structures collapse, and stability is replaced with uncertainty. For many Black Women, the workplace feels like an ongoing seismic event. Systems fail, plans fall apart, and eyes turn to *you* to clean it up, smooth it over, or make it right.

You didn't create the dysfunction.
You didn't hire the wrong people.
You didn't under-resource the team.
But now, you're expected to stabilize what others have shaken.

This isn't just frustrating—it's exhausting. It reinforces the false idea that your value lies in your ability to fix, carry, and endure, instead of your ability to lead, create, and transform.

"They will rebuild the ancient ruins and restore the places long devastated." — Isaiah 61:4 (NIV)

But rebuilding must be a shared responsibility—not a burden placed on one woman's shoulders.

In many organizations, Black women are asked to "represent diversity" and "heal team culture" without structural support, compensation, or positional authority—placing them in roles of silent repair. (Source: Harvard Business Review, 2022 – "Black Women and the Burden of Fixing Workplaces")

Activity 1: Reflection Prompt

"What have I been expected to fix that wasn't mine to break?"
"Where have I been assigned responsibility without authority?"

Write your reflections here:

Activity 2: Sort the Rubble

When an earthquake hits, not everything is worth rebuilding. Let's name what you've been holding—and decide what's yours to carry.

The Rubble I've Been Given	Was This My Responsibility?	Will I Keep Carrying It?
	Yes / No	Yes / No
	Yes / No	Yes / No
	Yes / No	Yes / No
	Yes / No	Yes / No
	Yes / No	Yes / No
	Yes / No	Yes / No

Releasing the "No" answers is not quitting. It's ***boundary work.***

Why It Matters for Black Women

Black women are often trained—by culture, family, faith, or survival—to fix everything and make everyone comfortable. But that conditioning leads to burnout, resentment, and invisibility.

Boundary work is how you stop proving, start preserving, and begin healing. It's how you move from survival mode to liberation.

What is Boundary Work?

Boundary work is the intentional practice of identifying what is and isn't yours to carry—and making choices that protect your time, energy, emotional health, and sense of self.

It's not about avoiding responsibility. It's about making sure you're not carrying other people's responsibilities, guilt, dysfunction, or emotional labor—especially when those burdens are silently handed to you.

Boundary Work Looks Like:

- **Saying "No"** to tasks outside your role that others could do for themselves.
- **Naming** that you are not responsible for fixing team dynamics without authority.
- **Deciding** that someone else's poor planning is not your emergency.
- **Releasing** the emotional labor of always being the one to de-escalate, explain, or translate things across cultures or roles.

- **Redirecting** responsibilities that belong to leadership, HR, or colleagues back to them.

Boundary Work Is NOT:

- Being rude or disengaged
- Refusing to collaborate
- Abandoning your role or sabotaging others
- “Quitting” in the sense of giving up—it’s strategic clarity

Activity 3: Mental Load Check-In

Check all that apply to you:

- I've been asked to fix team dynamics without formal leadership power.
- I've been asked to speak on behalf of all Black Women or "the culture."
- I'm asked to mediate or de-escalate conflict—often between others.
- I feel responsible for maintaining peace, even in toxic settings.
- I internalize guilt when I set boundaries or say no.
- (Other: ____)
- (Other: ____)
- (Other: ____)
- (Other: ____)

Activity 4: Purpose of a Reset Statement

What Is a Reset Statement?

A Reset Statement is a powerful declaration you speak, write, or reflect on to:

- Interrupt harmful thought patterns
- Reject internalized lies or expectations
- Realign with your truth, boundaries, and purpose

It's like hitting the mental and emotional "reset button" when the storm of expectations, microaggressions, or exhaustion has pulled you off course. Reset statements are short, bold, truth-filled, and empowering. They don't wait for permission. They return you to *your center*.

1. **Affirm Your Power**
   Reset statements remind you that you are not powerless—even when systems try to make you feel invisible or small.

2. **Challenge False Narratives**
   They help undo years of programming like:
   - *"If I don't fix it, no one will."*
   - *"I have to work twice as hard to be half as respected."*
   - *"Rest is lazy."*

3. **Protect Your Peace**
   When used regularly, they serve as a form of *mental boundary-setting*—reinforcing what you will and won't allow into your space.

4. **Ground You in Clarity**

   In moments of overwhelm, reset statements return your focus to what matters: your values, your well-being, and your worth.

When to Use a Reset Statement

Use a reset statement when:

- You feel overwhelmed, undervalued, or emotionally triggered.
- You're about to take on more than you should out of guilt or habit.
- You're second-guessing yourself in rooms where you belong.
- You need to reclaim your mental space before or after a hard conversation.
- You're trying to choose yourself, but old narratives are whispering otherwise.
- You're preparing for a meeting, review, or advocacy moment.

Write your own reset statement(s):

1. ____
2. ____
3. ____
4. ____
5. ____
6. ____

Activity 5: Truth Reset Statements

What is a Truth Reset Statement?

A Truth Reset Statement is a short, powerful declaration that helps you interrupt harmful thoughts, unlearn false expectations, and return to what's real.

It is your way of saying,

"This is what I know now."
"This is what I no longer accept."
"This is who I choose to be from this moment forward."

Truth Reset Statements are especially important when:

- You've internalized beliefs that are no longer serving you
- You've been performing, over-functioning, or shrinking to be accepted
- You need a mental and emotional boundary between *who you are* and *what the world expects you to be*

These are not just affirmations; they are clarifying, cleansing, truth-telling sentences that pull you back to your power and remind you of your value.

Use them when:

- You feel unseen, overworked, or underappreciated
- You're tempted to downplay your credentials or shrink your presence
- You're in a space where labor is expected but not rewarded
- You need to reset the narrative in your mind and spirit

Remember:

You don't have to believe the lie to be affected by it.
A Truth Reset Statement gives you language to push back—with clarity, compassion, and conviction.

Write your own or complete these:

1. I no longer carry what does not belong to me.
2. I do not need to prove my worth through labor others avoid.
3. My peace is more important than their perception.
4. ____
5. ____
6. ____

Reset Statement vs. Truth Reset Statement

Reset Statement	Truth Reset Statement
Helps you emotionally regulate in a moment of stress or overload	Helps you reject a false belief and reaffirm your identity and worth
Short-term clarity	Long-term truth alignment
E.g., "I can pause before I respond."	E.g., "I no longer prove my worth through overworking."

Both types of statements are vital tools. One brings you back to center. The other brings you back to the truth.

Activity 6: Affirmation

What you say to yourself is important; your words will refresh your brain, body, and soul. Say it!

Read it!

Affirmation

"I release the pressure to be the fixer.
I release the lie that I am responsible for what others broke.
I am not here to hold up cracked foundations.
I build where I am called—and I rest where I am not."

Write It!

____

____

____

Write It!

____

____

____

Write It!

____

____

____

SINKHOLE OF SELF-WORTH: WHEN STRESS BECOMES IDENTITY

"I am not what I survived. I am who I am becoming."

Reflection

What have I buried that I now want to reclaim?

____

____

____

What do I want to stop doing to prove my worth?

____

____

____

I release the lie that I am only valuable when I am performing.

I stand on solid ground
I honor who I am becoming.

Sinkhole of Self-Worth: When Stress Becomes Identity

"If I'm not doing everything... Who am I?"

Sinkholes appear without warning. They form beneath the surface, eroding the ground bit by bit until everything collapses. For many Black Women, the workplace becomes a silent erosion of identity. Years of being overlooked, undervalued, and overextended wear down your sense of self.

You begin to confuse busyness with value, exhaustion with excellence, overwork with success.
You feel guilty for resting.
You struggle to separate your worth from your performance.
You ask: *If I stop doing everything, will I still matter?*

This isn't just burnout. This is identity loss. And it is not your fault.

"You are precious in my eyes, and honored, and I love you." — Isaiah 43:4 (ESV)

You were never created to be the chaos cleaner, the crisis handler, or the cultural translator for everyone. You are not the glue. You are the gold.

It's time to reclaim your worth - apart from how much you carry.

Black women are more likely to suffer from "strong Black woman schema," a cultural and psychological pressure to suppress vulnerability, over-function, and define self-worth through caregiving and endurance.

(Source: American Psychological Association, 2022)

Activity 1: Reflection Prompt

1. "What roles or patterns have I taken on that are not aligned with who I truly am?"
2. "What have I believed about myself because of how others treated me?"

Write your reflections here:

Activity 2: Separate Self from Stress

Draw two overlapping circles or use the table below to distinguish who you are vs. what you've been conditioned to do.

Who I Am	**What I've Been Conditioned to Do**
______________________	Always say yes
______________________	Be twice as good for half the recognition
______________________	Be the calm, the fixer, the forgiver, the glue

Now choose one behavior to release this week. Write a new truth to replace it.

____

____

____

____

____

____

____

____

____

Activity 3: Reset and Release

Complete or create your own:

I am not my workload

I am more than how much I do for others.

My rest is not a reward—it is a right.

Activity 4: Affirmation

What you say to yourself is important; your words will refresh your brain, body, and soul. Say it!

Read it!

"I release the lie that I must constantly perform to be worthy.
I was valuable before the degree, the job, the titles.
I am worthy of love, visibility, and rest.
I return to myself—and that is more than enough."

Write It!

Write It!

Write It!

The Forecast: You Are the Calm, Not the Storm

"I can't control the weather. But I can decide how I show up in it."

After tornadoes, typhoons, floods, hurricanes, earthquakes, and sinkholes, what's left?

You.

Not broken.
Not buried.
Still standing.

The storms didn't define you. They revealed you. And what was revealed is this: you are not chaos, you are clarity.

You've named the systems. You've released what wasn't yours to carry. You've drawn the line between proving and preserving, between exhaustion and identity.

Now, it's time to write your own weather report—to set the forecast for how you'll move forward.

Activity 1: Reflection Prompt: Reclaiming the Atmosphere

Use the space below to speak power into your future.

"From this point forward, I will no longer…"

"I give myself permission to…"

"I will protect my peace by…"

Activity 2: Write Your Weather Report

Describe the atmosphere you want to live, work, and thrive in from this moment forward.

Old Climate	*New Forecast*
High-pressure demands	Gentle boundaries and grace
Unrelenting visibility hunger	Confidence without overexposure
Chronic over-functioning	Rest as resistance and restoration
Being the fixer of others' failures	Empowering others to be accountable

Now, write a few lines describing the *forecast* for your life, your energy, your work, your wellness.

"The climate I now choose is…"

____

____

____

____

____

Activity 3: Final Affirmation: Speak Your Calm

Say It! - Read It!

"I do not chase storms to prove I'm strong.
I do not wear stress like a badge.
I operate in clarity, not chaos.
I am the calm. I am the shift.
I am the forecast I've been waiting for."

Write It!

Write It!

Write It!

Chapter 2

Internal Chaos

Chapter 2 – Internal Chaos

Introduction

I recently read an Instagram post that stated the female flamingo will lose its color. Why? As the mother, she pours so much of herself into her children, family, etc, others that she actually loses her color in the process. This was significant to me, as we consider the type and level of internal chaos that we operate within. What is draining your pink, the very essence of who you are? What internalized chaos are you operating in that is causing you to lose the ability to self-love, self-care, and soul care that is going to enhance your spirit?

What is internal chaos? Internal chaos is the state of being that we often find ourselves operating within when our emotions, thoughts, and feelings begin to collide and create turmoil. That turmoil is such that it adversely impacts our life, our peace is disturbed, we find it hard to concentrate, to focus on even the most mundane circumstances. Internal chaos can manifest in various forms within individuals or organizations. These types of internal chaos can significantly impact productivity and well-being, highlighting the importance of addressing them proactively.

Factors of Internal Chaos

Five common types of internal chaos that might be at work in you:

1. Emotional Turmoil
2. Cognitive Overload
3. Relationship Conflicts
4. Lack of Direction/Self-Esteem
5. Disorganization

Emotional Turmoil

This involves feelings of anxiety, stress, or confusion that disrupt mental regulation. Origins may include personal issues, work pressures, or unresolved conflicts. Stress, diet changes, and environmental factors also cause internal chaos, and what is depleting you.

How do you know when something is triggering you internally? Let's begin with a short exercise that will let you see what is stirring around on the inside.

Activity 1: What is on the inside?

1. Intensity: On a scale of 1 (less intense) -5 (most intense), I am at a

   __________.

2. Duration: On average, I feel this way ________________________________

   ____

   ____

   ____

3. Disruption: When I begin to feel this way, it affects my life:

   □ Every Day □ Occasionally □ Never

4. Confusion: I feel out of sorts and have a hard time making sense of my feelings.

   □ True □ False

5. Physical symptoms: My body feels

   ____

   ____

   ____

   ____

Cognitive Overload

Have You Lost Your Identity?

This occurs when an individual faces too much information or too many tasks at once, leading to difficulty in decision-making and prioritization. This happens when the individual is constantly torn between who she is and who she wishes to be.

Functional depression is an indicator that can create the loss of identity, the loss of motivation, the lack of interest in self and others. Although you work, joke around, and take care of people around you. But mentally, you are drowning in your own thoughts, and nobody knows it.

Activity 1: Let's look in the mirror

Mirror, mirror on the wall, I see:

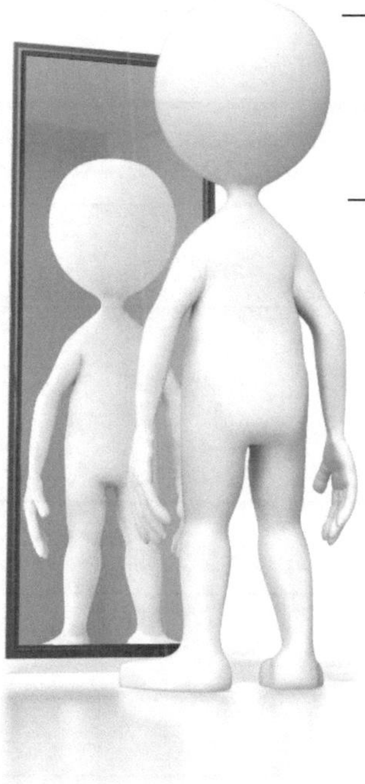

Relationship Conflicts

Disagreements or misunderstandings among family members, miscommunication, hurt feelings, poverty, anxiety, colleagues, and even romantic partners can create a chaotic environment, affecting not only the relationship but the individual's inner conflict about the relationship.

Activity 1: Inner Conflict about Relationships

When I think about my family relationships, I feel they are:

____

____

____

____

When I think about my romantic relationships, I feel:

____

____

____

____

When I think about my work relationships, I feel:

____

____

____

____

Lack of Direction/Self-Esteem

When goals are unclear or constantly changing, individuals may feel lost or unmotivated, lacking in self-worth thereby contributing to a sense of chaos in their work or personal life. Let's put a label on it as Imposter syndrome. Imposter syndrome can be defined as lack of self-confidence, self-worth, or lacking competence.

Activity 1: Imposter Syndrome

My Imposter syndrome shows up as:

Disorganization

Physical or digital clutter can lead to inefficiency and frustration. A disorganized environment makes it challenging to focus and complete tasks effectively.

'A cluttered house is indicative of a cluttered mind'.

How many times have we heard that old adage. Our lives are representative of our homes, etc... Have you heard yourself say *'once I get my house in order, I'll feel better'*. This is often true, because when we are surrounded by clutter, internalizing the chaotic thoughts and feelings we are disorganized (externally) and dysregulated (internally).

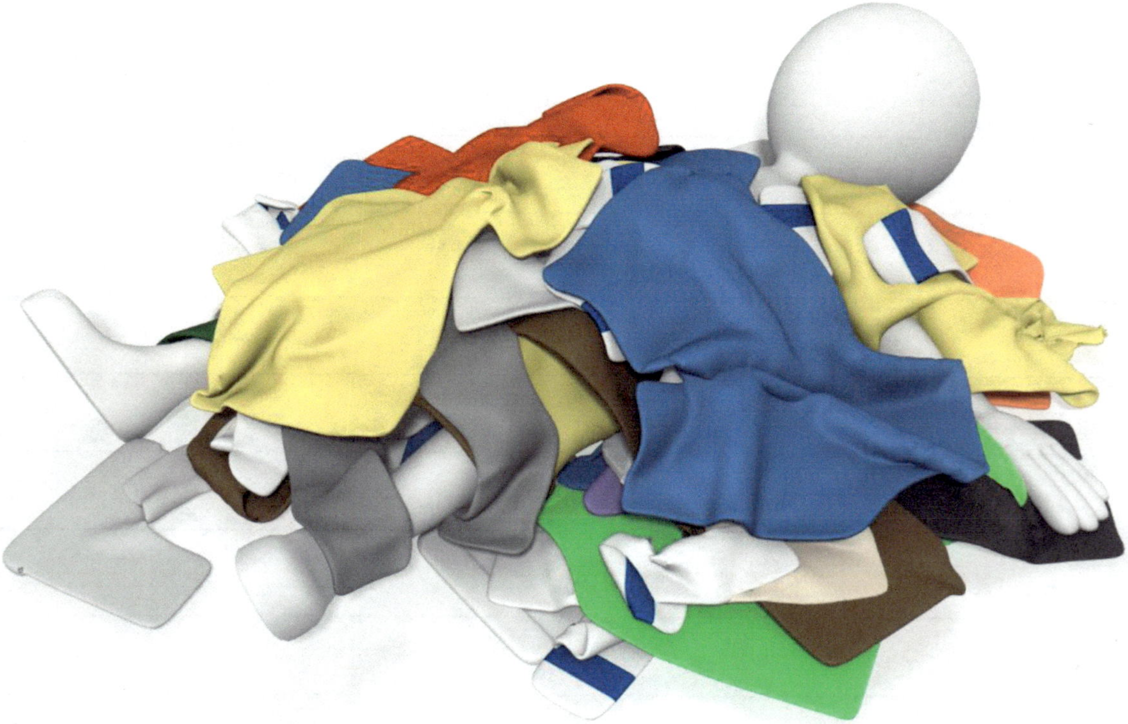

Activity 1: My House

Right now, my house holds:

When was the last time you took an intentional breath? Not the breath that demonstrates exasperation over the last email you read, or the loud, exhausting sigh of disgust. We tend to live in the short and shallow, meaning we automatically breathe, and thankfully so. We get up in the morning, feet hit the floor, and we INHALE.. Next is the busyness of the day that quickly ensues.... Fixing breakfast, taking the children to school, getting ready for work, answering email, the telephone and navigating the many relationships that present themselves during the day. When did you EXHALE.... Not out of exhaustion or exasperation, ...the intentional cleansing breath just because you are worthy and have earned it.

Activity 2: Breathe

Let's start here. First, find your comfortable, safe place. Place your hands and feet solidly on a flat surface, and close your eyes. You may also place one hand on your chest and one hand on your diaphragm. Now focus on that breath, inhale through your nose 1, 2, 3, 4, 5 HOLD, now slowly exhale through your mouth.

Activity 3: Remember your joy

Joy is defined as a state of great pleasure or happiness. One would offer that joy is not easily moved, a foundational or core state. Do you have JOY? Describe it below:

____

____

____

____

____

Now, describe what you want your joy to look like.

____

____

____

____

____

____

List 3 ways in which you will practice joy or joyful behavior.

1. ____
2. ____
3. ____

Speak Life

Speak life over yourself. The way you speak to yourself matters. Have you ever found yourself getting caught in a negative loop, repeating words, thoughts, and feelings that keep you down? There are occasions when we unintentionally feed the conflict or turmoil that we are experiencing.

Activity 1: What does it sound like?

Write down what that tape sounds like.....

____

____

____

Now, it is time to change the tape. List 3 ways in which you will speak life over yourself.

1. ____
2. ____
3. ____

"Death and life are in the power of the tongue, And those who love it will eat its fruit." — Proverbs 18:21 (NKJV)

Enrich Your Diet

Feed yourself, mentally, physically, and spiritually.

When we use the word diet, typically, one thinks of shedding pounds. A diet can also be described as 'the regulation of' when we use the word in the verb tense, when used as an adjective, a diet is 'a part of'; when used as a noun, a diet is a 'particular selection'. So let's look at our mental, physical, and spiritual diet.

Activity 1: Physical Diet

Select which of the groups are included in your **Physical** diet.

Activity 2: Mental Diet

Select which of the groups are included in your **Mental** diet include:

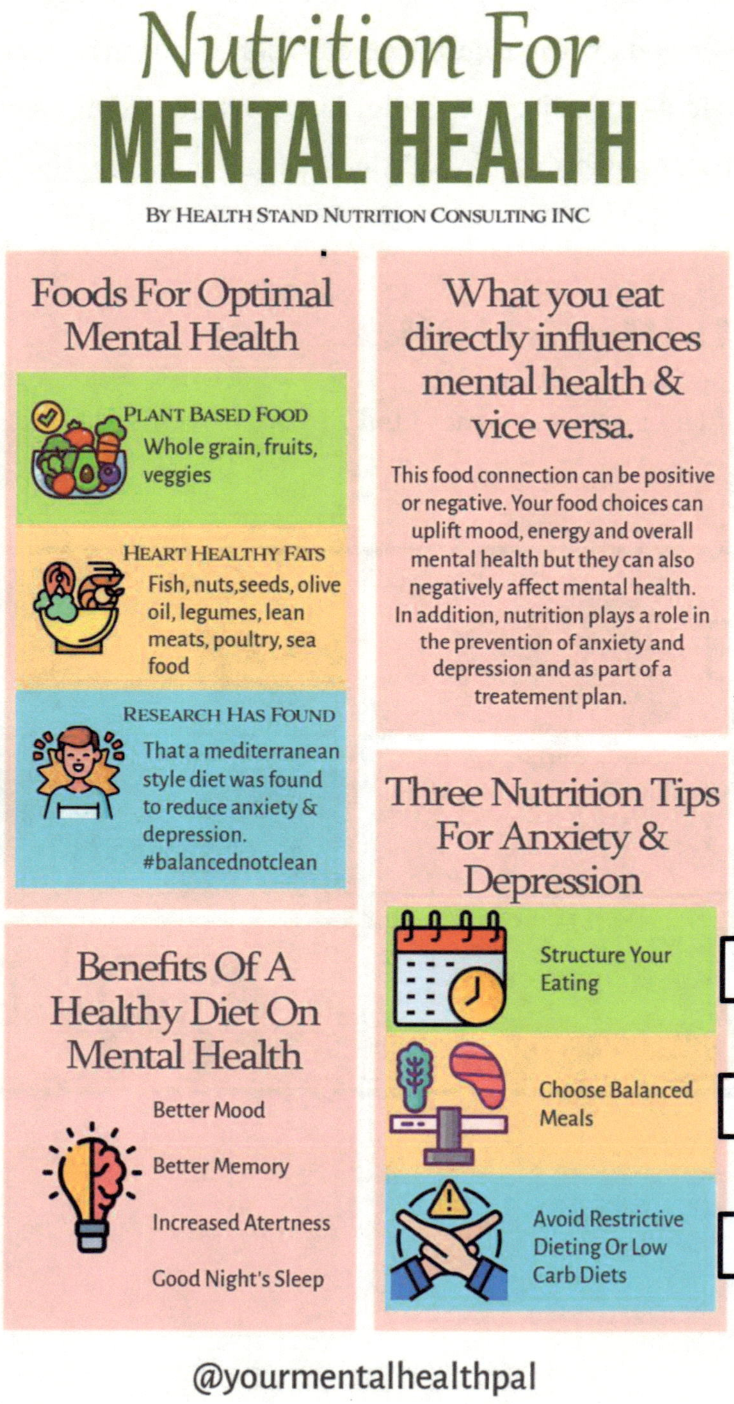

Plant Based Food: □ Yes □ No

Heart Healthy Fats: □ Yes □ No

Research Has Found: □ Yes □ No

Structure Your Eating: □ Yes □ No

Choose Balanced Meals: □ Yes □ No

Avoid Restrictive Dieting Or Low Carb Diets: □ Yes □ No

Activity 3: My Physical and Mental Diet

What, from the above groups, will I begin to use or continue to use in my Physical and Mental Diet?

Physical Diet	Mental Diet

Activity 4: Spiritual Diet

Right now, does my **Spiritual** diet include a belief system of one greater than me? Am I providing myself with the soul care, meaning, the opportunity to nurture or nourish my inner being, and intentionally give attention to that area of my life that requires healing?

My soul needs:

____

____

____

____

____

____

List 3 ways in which you will provide more Soul care:

1. ______________________________

2. ______________________________

3. ______________________________

It's not your season. **Let it go.**

We tend to hold onto things in attempts to revive and resuscitate them. We were designed to provide care, support,

____

____

____

____

____

____

What are the top 3 things you need to release? Remember, you may be delayed and not denied.

1. ______________________________
2. ______________________________
3. ______________________________

IT'S NOT YOUR SEASON......

YET.

Activity 5: Healthy relationship(s).

Nourish the healthy relationship(s) you have cultivated. A healthy relationship is often characterized by respect, communication, trust, honesty, empathy, respect for others' boundaries, kindness, affection, and support.

When I think of my current relationships, I see the following:

____

____

____

____

____

____

List 3 ways in which you will practice having a healthy relationship(s).

1. ____
2. ____
3. ____

Appreciate Yourself

Prioritize; stop multitasking and feeding the chaos; be gracious to yourself. Remember you have the ability to make informed, educated decisions. Remember, it is okay to celebrate yourself in spite of the current situation.

I forgot to appreciate myself when....

____

____

____

____

____

List 3 ways in which you will practice appreciation.

1. ____

2. ____

3. ____

"Love yourself, appreciate yourself, see the good in you... and respect yourself."

- Betty Shabazz

Let Your Light Shine

Improve your posture. Stand up! in who you have been created to be. Don't let imposter syndrome attack your esteem and cause you to doubt. Be authentic with your actions, as you are the model for others.

I dimmed my light when....

____

____

____

____

____

List 3 ways in which you will let your light shine:

1. ____

2. ____

3. ____

You better walk into that room like God sent you in there!

Chapter 3 Managing Internal & External Chaos

Chapter 3 – Managing Internal & External Chaos

Introduction

Chaos shows up in many forms, unexpected changes, competing priorities, shifting demands, or the simple weight of too much happening at once. It can scatter your focus, drain your energy, and make even simple decisions feel heavy. Chaos regardless of its origin (external or internal) exists because of turmoil, disorder, confusion, lack of organization, and other noticeable behaviors due to the absence of calm. Managing external and internal chaos begins with understanding their meanings, differences, and similarities. The understanding offers an opportunity to manage the chaos day-to-day life brings.

This chapter is designed to help you regain your balance. It offers structure where things feel uncertain, perspective where things feel overwhelming, and practical tools to help you move from reaction to intention. You're not here to chase perfection. You're here to create clarity. You're not here to eliminate every challenge. You're here to navigate them with confidence. Let this be your starting point, a space to slow down, sort through the noise, and build a more grounded way forward.

Being able to manage the chaos day-to-day life means first acknowledging there is chaos, then naming the chaos, compartmentalizing the chaos as external or internal, identifying the areas in day-to-day life where chaos resides, identifying the behavior associated with the identified chaos, determining actions required to minimize or eliminate the chaos, and setting actionable goals to minimize and/or eliminate the chaos.

Journaling has proven to be therapeutic and provides clarity. After each area there is space to take notes **(Journal of Thoughts)** on your thoughts regarding how you see yourself in each space. In general, share what you're thinking in that space and come back later to explore what it looks like now and in the future.

Acknowledge There is Chaos

CHAOS Acknowledgement

I ____ being of sound, mind, and body, do solemnly swear that I am acknowledging that I have not been coerced to say that I recognize I have chaos in my life and that I am ready, willing, and able to begin managing said chaos in my life.

I affirm that:

_______ I acknowledge there is chaos in my life.

_______ The chaos in my life is both internal and external.

_______ I am ready, willing, and able to invest the time to identify the areas in my day-to-day life where chaos resides.

_______ I am willing to invest the time required to name the chaos in my day-to-day life.

_______ I am open to identifying the behavior I exhibit when there is chaos in my day-to-day life.

_______ I am committed to taking action to eliminate or minimize the chaos in my day-to-day life.

_______ I am committed to setting and managing the goals associated with eliminating and or minimizing chaos in my day-to-day life.

I declare under penalty of failing to manage the chaos in my day-to-day life that the foregoing is true and initialed with true intentions and commitment; correct to the best of my knowledge and belief.

____ Printed Name

____ Signature

____ Date

Commitment Statement

Now that you have acknowledged that there is chaos and you are ready to manage it, let's write a short commitment statement. Use the template below to begin writing what your commitment statement to managing chaos looks like.

Template:

"I commit to leading myself with clarity and courage. I honor my limits, protect my peace, and choose order over overwhelm. I am not ruled by chaos — I shape it."

Journal of Thoughts

Journal of Thoughts

Naming Chaos

Naming Your Chaos

In exploring the landscape of chaos, it is essential to understand not only the terminology but also the behaviors, both negative and positive, that arise when chaos manifests, whether externally or internally. External chaos may be observable in the world around us: in our environments, relationships, and organizations. Internal chaos, meanwhile, is experienced within, shaping thoughts, reactions, and emotional states. Recognizing the words we use to describe these forms of chaos, and the spectrum of behaviors they provoke, equips us to navigate and ultimately transform disorder into clarity and growth.

The experience of chaos often has a look or feel. The look or feel is associated with a positive or negative behavior. Understanding the type of negative behavior associated with the chaos you are experiencing, will provide you with the information needed to understand what behavior will be exhibited once the chaos is managed. Let's look at the example on the next page to name the negative behavior associated with your day-to-day activities.

The experience of chaos often has a look or feel. The look or feel is associated with a positive or negative behavior. Understanding the type of negative behavior associated with the chaos you are experiencing, will provide you with the information needed to understand what behavior will be exhibited once the chaos is managed. Let's look at the example below to name the negative behavior associated with your day-to-day activities.

Example:

What does chaos look or feel like? Clutter.

Statement of what it looks or feels like: My chaos looks like clutter.

Naming what chaos looks and feels like, leads to the where, why, and how of the behavior associated with the named chaos. On the next page, the negative behaviors associated with clutter look or feel like untidiness, mess, disorder, confusion, imbalance, a hodgepodge, and litter. Dissecting the behavior answers the where, why, and how of the behavior .

Where is the clutter? My office

How do you know it is chaos? My office is messy

How does the chaos limit you? I can't think

Why is the limitation important? I am confused and cannot form cohesive thoughts

Statement of the where, why, and how of the chaos: My office is messy and I cannot think amongst the mess.

Basically, naming the chaos allows for the understanding of how a cluttered office limits one's ability to form cohesive thoughts. Along with the negative behaviors of clutter, there are the positive behaviors of order, organization, singularity, and system once the clutter is no longer visible. So, once the clutter is cleared, the chaos is managed, and the positive behavior of the chaos statement is: Clearing up the clutter will allow for clarity and organization.

Now, it's time to name your chaos. Use the Terms and Behaviors associated with External and Internal Chaos tables to complete the Naming your chaos worksheet(s). The blank rows in the tables are for you to name behaviors that you have recognized or will recognize day-to-day.

Activity 1: Naming Your Chaos

What does chaos look or feel like? ______________________________________

Statement of what it looks or feels like: _________________________________

____

____

Naming what chaos looks and feels like, leads to the **where, why, and how** of the behavior associated with the named chaos.

Where is the clutter? ____

____

How do you know it is chaos? ____

____

How does the chaos limit you? ____

____

Why is the limitation important? _______________________________________

____

Statement of the where, why, and how of the chaos:

____

____

____

____

____

Activity 1: Naming Your Chaos

What does chaos look or feel like? ______________________________________

Statement of what it looks or feels like: ______________________________

____

____

Naming what chaos looks and feels like, leads to the **where, why, and how** of the behavior associated with the named chaos.

Where is the clutter? ____

____

How do you know it is chaos? ______________________________________

____

How does the chaos limit you? _____________________________________

____

Why is the limitation important? ___________________________________

____

Statement of the where, why, and how of the chaos:

____

____

____

____

____

Activity 1: Naming Your Chaos

What does chaos look or feel like? ______________________________

Statement of what it looks or feels like: ______________________________

____

____

Naming what chaos looks and feels like, leads to the **where, why, and how** of the behavior associated with the named chaos.

Where is the clutter? ______________________________

____

How do you know it is chaos? ______________________________

____

How does the chaos limit you? ______________________________

____

Why is the limitation important? ______________________________

____

Statement of the where, why, and how of the chaos:

____

____

____

____

____

Activity 1: Naming Your Chaos

What does chaos look or feel like? ______________________________

Statement of what it looks or feels like: ______________________________

____

____

Naming what chaos looks and feels like, leads to the **where, why, and how** of the behavior associated with the named chaos.

Where is the clutter? ______________________________

____

How do you know it is chaos? ______________________________

____

How does the chaos limit you? ______________________________

____

Why is the limitation important? ______________________________

____

Statement of the where, why, and how of the chaos:

____

____

____

____

____

Terms and Behaviors associated with YOUR External and Internal Chaos

What the Experience of Chaos **Looks/Feels** Like	**Negative** Behaviors Associated with What Chaos **Looks/Feels** Like	**Positive** Behaviors Associated with What Chaos **Looks/Feels** Like
Anarchy	Confusion, lawlessness, rebellion, insurrection	Calm, method, organization, structure
Animosity	Bitterness, hate, hostility, resentment, anger	Rapport, respect, kindness, sympathy
Avoidance	Working long hours, taking on more than they can accomplish, always busy, can't commit	Reduce working hours, more free time for self, friends, and family
Ataxia	Entropy, free-for-all, misrule, mix up	Normality, neatness, orderliness, tidiness
Bedlam	Clamor, commotion, furor, hubbub	Harmony, peace, silence, system
Bitterness	Anger, resentment, outbursts, verbal or physical aggression	Calm, introspection
Clutter	Untidiness, mess, disorder, confusion, derangement, hodgepodge, litter	Order, organization, singularity, system
Disarray	Clutter, disorganization, jumble, untidiness	Harmony, tidiness, order, neatness
Discord	Disharmony, dissonance, harshness, tumult,	Accord, agreement, concord, harmony
Disorder	Irregularity, jumble, mess, shambles, confusion	Method, organization, rule, system
Disorganization	Inefficiency, incompetence, ineffectiveness, ineptitude, lack of ability, lack of skill	Arrangement, coherence, method, plan

Terms and Behaviors associated with YOUR External and Internal Chaos

What the Experience of Chaos **Looks/Feels** Like	**Negative** Behaviors Associated with What Chaos **Looks/Feels** Like	**Positive** Behaviors Associated with What Chaos **Looks/Feels** Like
Entropy	Breakup, collapse, decay, decline	Improvement, increase, rise
Fear	Anger, bitterness, stress	
Fickleness	Unsurety, questions everything	
Free-for-all	Misrule, mix up, snarl, unruliness	Neatness, normality, quiet, system
Insecurity	Paranoia, mistrust, suspicion	
Lack of self-worth	Helplessness, hopelessness, despair	Mantras of positivity and self-worth
Lawlessness	Confusion, disorder, terrorism	Calm, method, organization, system
Misrule	Discombobulation, shambles, mess, snarl	Method, order, system, tidiness
Mix-up	Botch, jumble, mistake, tangle	Peace, quiet, system, understanding
Mobocracy	Holy mess, rat's nest, topsy-turviness	Ease, orderliness, neatness, normality, system
Muddle	Encumbrance hash, haze, predicament	Enlightenment, good fortune, simplicity,
Negativity	Intentionally inciting or intensifying arguments unnecessarily	Walking away from arguments

Terms and Behaviors associated with YOUR External and Internal Chaos

What the Experience of Chaos **Looks/Feels** Like	**Negative** Behaviors Associated with What Chaos **Looks/Feels** Like	**Positive** Behaviors Associated with What Chaos **Looks/Feels** Like
Pandemonium	Bedlam, brouhaha, ruckus, uproar	Calm, order, peace, quiet
Self-Important	Needy, manipulative, lack of empathy for others	
Snarl	Complexity, intricacy, maze, web	Ease, orderliness, simplicity, system
Stress	Restlessness, over-eating, under-eating, binge-eating	Relaxation, me time, pick your battles
Uncommunicative	Unclear instructions, messaging confusing, unable to build trust	Listen to understand
Unruliness	Fractiousness, impulsiveness, intractability, wildness	Carefulness, caution, modesty, politeness
Tumult	Agitation, disturbance, maelstrom, quarrel	Agreement, calmness, stillness, tranquility
Turmoil	Agitation, anxiousness, disquiet, anxiety	Calm, tranquil, peace, silence

Activity 2: Terms and Behaviors associated with YOUR External and Internal Chaos

Use this table to add the **experience of Chaos** and their behaviors you have experienced or learned about.

What the Experience of Chaos **Looks/Feels** Like	**Negative** Behaviors Associated with What Chaos **Looks/Feels** Like	**Positive** Behaviors Associated with What Chaos **Looks/Feels** Like

Journal of Thoughts

Use this area to document your thoughts and next actions for **Terms and Behaviors associated with YOUR External and Internal Chaos**.

Journal of Thoughts

Journal of Thoughts

Identifying the Source of Chaos

Identifying the Source of Chaos

Before delving into the causes of chaos, it is crucial to clarify the various terms and categories that shape our understanding of disorder. Chaos can emerge from a wide spectrum of sources, both external and internal, each carrying distinct characteristics and implications. By carefully identifying and defining these associated terms, we lay the groundwork for a deeper exploration of what chaos is, how it manifests, and the factors that contribute to its presence across different areas of life. This clarity not only aids in recognizing chaos in its many forms, but also empowers us to address it more effectively.

The source of the chaos can be external or internal individually, or it can be a combination of both. To identify the type of chaos, we are going to use (external, internal, or both) and then its source (self, work, family, political, religious, and/or other). Let's take a closer look at each of these and how they are used to assist with identifying chaos's source.

Types of Chaos

- External - this are actions that are due to outside forces you cannot control, yet they become chaos
- Internal - mental instability, emotional anguish, brain never resting because of continuous anxiety
- Both - a combination of both

Sources of Chaos

- Self
- Work
- Family
- Political
- Religious
- Other

The Activity below is part of your journey in being able to recognize the chaos in your life and where it comes from. Being able to identify where the chaos originates will enable you to begin managing and controlling the chaos you allow in your life.

To complete the table, identify whether the chaos is internal or external, then identify its source. Remember it can be internal or external and it can come from different sources.

Activity 1: Identifying the Source Chaos

Use this table to identify the type of chaos and the **source of chaos** as it relates to the "What Chaos Looks Like".

Types of Chaos		Source of Chaos					
What Chaos Looks Like	External / Internal / Both	Self	Work	Family	Political	Religious	Other
Anarchy							
Animosity							
Ataxia							
Bedlam							
Bitterness							
Clutter							
Disarray							
Discord							
Disorder							
Disorganization							
Entropy							
Fear							
Fickleness							
Free-For-All							

Types of Chaos		Source of Chaos					
What Chaos Looks Like	External / Internal / Both	Self	Work	Family	Political	Religious	Other
Insecurity							
Lack of self worth							
Lawlessness							
Misrule							
Mix-up							
Mobocracy							
Muddle							
Negativity							
Pandemonium							
Self-Important							
Snarl							
Stress							
Uncommunicative							
Tumult							

Types of Chaos		Source of Chaos					
What Chaos Looks Like	External / Internal / Both	Self	Work	Family	Political	Religious	Other
Turmoil							

Journal of Thoughts

Use this area to document your thoughts and next actions for **Terms and Behaviors associated with YOUR External and Internal Chaos**.

Journal of Thoughts

Journal of Thoughts

Your Role in the Chaos

Now that you have identified the source of the chaos, let's look at what role your behavior put you in. Use the empty rows to identify other roles not mentioned. Refer back to this activity in the future to ensure you **DO NOT** fill a role that creates chaos in your day-to-day life.

The **role** you filled	How it **added chaos** to your space	What your **chaotic behavior** looked like
The Problem Solver	Everything was a problem for you to solve	Responsive, weak and tired
The Performer	Someone always wants your attention	Always doing something for others
The Helper	Available anytime	Rushing, never on schedule
The Creative Thinker	Always offering assistance with ideas	Frenzied
The Procrastinator	Putting things off	Postponement

Activity 2: Your Role in the Chaos

Use the table below to identify the chaotic behavior you exhibited and how it added chaos to your space when you were in one of the roles discussed in the previous activity.

What Chaotic Behavior Look(ed) Like	How it added chaos to your space	The Role
Frenzy		
Stress		

Journal of Thoughts

Use this area to document your thoughts and next actions for **managing the role** you play in the chaos in your day-to-day activities.

Journal of Thoughts

Journal of Thoughts

Quieting the Chaos

Ways to Quiet or Eliminate Chaos

Chaos can arise unexpectedly, disrupting routines, testing our patience, and clouding our sense of calm. Whether it stems from external circumstances, emotional turbulence, or the complexities of modern living, chaos can feel overwhelming. Yet, within the noise and disorder, there exist pathways to peace and resilience. By exploring and applying practical strategies, be they internal or external, or a combination of both, we empower ourselves to quiet the clamor, minimize its impact, and sometimes eliminate chaos altogether.

By completing the activity below. You will be presented with a variety of approaches, helping you discover ways to restore equilibrium, foster clarity, and reclaim a sense of control amidst the storm.

Activity 1: Ways to Quiet or Eliminate Chaos

Use the table to identify how you cope with chaos.

Coping looks like		How can coping be used…					
Type of Coping Mechanism	External / Internal / Both	Self	Work	Family	Political	Religious	Other
Breathing							
Cleaning up as I go							
Exercising / Yoga							
Ignoring Noise							
Me Time							
Meditating							
Night Out (Girls or Guys)							
Praying							
Putting things in their places							
Quiet							
Reading							
Recognizing my triggers							
Running / Walking							
Solitude							

Activity 2: Ways You Quiet or Eliminate Chaos

Use this table to add **coping mechanisms you have used or plan to use to QUIET or ELIMINATE Chaos.**

Coping looks like		How can coping be used…					
Type of Coping Mechanism	External / Internal / Both	Self	Work	Family	Political	Religious	Other

Journal of Thoughts

Use this area to take notes on different **ways you can quiet or eliminate chaos.**

Journal of Thoughts

Journal of Thoughts

MANAGING THE CHAOS

Managing Chaos

In any environment, personal, professional, or communal, chaos can arrive unannounced, disrupting the patterns we rely on and testing the strength of our resolve. Yet within every disordered moment lies a blueprint for renewed clarity and control. This chapter gathers practical strategies, insightful reflections, and time-tested tools to guide you through the turbulence. By thoughtfully applying each concept and lesson outlined here, you will not only weather the storms of chaos but learn to transform them into opportunities for purposeful action and lasting calmness. Let us now explore how to move from disorder to direction, harnessing every insight within these pages to create order where there was once uncertainty.

Activity 1: Working Through and Managing

Working through and managing is designed for you to identify the chaos and determine what you are willing to do to eliminate or minimize the chaos in your life.

"**Notes to Self**" is similar to the "**Journal of Thoughts**", however, it focuses on the chaos you are working through in the activity. Use the area for notes you want to refer back to when dealing that specific type of chaos.

Activity 1: Working Through and Managing Chaos

What Chaos looks like ____

Is the Chaos ☐ External ☐ Internal ☐ Both

What caused the Chaos ☐ Self ☐ Work ☐ Family ☐ Political ☐ Religious

Other ____

The negative behavior (perception - what is seen or felt) of the chaos

____

____

____

Positive behavior you want to experience or perceived

____

____

____

I will manage ________________________ by purposefully recognizing when ______________ happens or is manifesting in negative behavior. To ensure success, I will ______________________ to clear or remove the chaos I am experiencing.

As a reminder, I will pay attention to the things below, to aid in my management of chaos.

What Negative Behavior Looks Like	What may Trigger the Negative Behavior	What action will mitigate Negative Behavior

Notes to Self

Activity 1: Working Through and Managing Chaos

What Chaos looks like ____

Is the Chaos ☐ External ☐ Internal ☐ Both

What caused the Chaos ☐ Self ☐ Work ☐ Family ☐ Political ☐ Religious

Other ____

The negative behavior (perception - what is seen or felt) of the chaos

____

____

____

Positive behavior you want to experience or perceived

____

____

____

I will manage ________________________ by purposefully recognizing when _______________ happens or is manifesting in negative behavior. To ensure success, I will ______________________ to clear or remove the chaos I am experiencing.

As a reminder, I will pay attention to the things below, to aid in my management of chaos.

What Negative Behavior Looks Like	What may Trigger the Negative Behavior	What action will mitigate Negative Behavior

Notes to Self

Activity 1: Working Through and Managing Chaos

What Chaos looks like ____

Is the Chaos ☐ External ☐ Internal ☐ Both

What caused the Chaos ☐ Self ☐ Work ☐ Family ☐ Political ☐ Religious

Other ____

The negative behavior (perception - what is seen or felt) of the chaos

____

____

____

Positive behavior you want to experience or perceived

____

____

____

I will manage ______________________ by purposefully recognizing when ______________ happens or is manifesting in negative behavior. To ensure success, I will ____________________ to clear or remove the chaos I am experiencing.

As a reminder, I will pay attention to the things below, to aid in my management of chaos.

What Negative Behavior Looks Like	What may Trigger the Negative Behavior	What action will mitigate Negative Behavior

Notes to Self

Activity 1: Working Through and Managing Chaos

What Chaos looks like ____

Is the Chaos ☐ External ☐ Internal ☐ Both

What caused the Chaos ☐ Self ☐ Work ☐ Family ☐ Political ☐ Religious

Other ____

The negative behavior (perception - what is seen or felt) of the chaos

____

____

____

Positive behavior you want to experience or perceived

____

____

____

I will manage ________________________ by purposefully recognizing when ______________ happens or is manifesting in negative behavior. To ensure success, I will ______________________ to clear or remove the chaos I am experiencing.

As a reminder, I will pay attention to the things below, to aid in my management of chaos.

What Negative Behavior Looks Like	What may Trigger the Negative Behavior	What action will mitigate Negative Behavior

Notes to Self

Activity 1: Working Through and Managing Chaos

What Chaos looks like ____

Is the Chaos ☐ External ☐ Internal ☐ Both

What caused the Chaos ☐ Self ☐ Work ☐ Family ☐ Political ☐ Religious

Other ____

The negative behavior (perception - what is seen or felt) of the chaos

____

____

____

Positive behavior you want to experience or perceived

____

____

____

I will manage ________________________ by purposefully recognizing when ______________ happens or is manifesting in negative behavior. To ensure success, I will ______________________ to clear or remove the chaos I am experiencing.

As a reminder, I will pay attention to the things below, to aid in my management of chaos.

What Negative Behavior Looks Like	What may Trigger the Negative Behavior	What action will mitigate Negative Behavior

Notes to Self

Activity 1: Working Through and Managing Chaos

What Chaos looks like ____

Is the Chaos ☐ External ☐ Internal ☐ Both

What caused the Chaos ☐ Self ☐ Work ☐ Family ☐ Political ☐ Religious

Other ____

The negative behavior (perception - what is seen or felt) of the chaos

____

____

____

Positive behavior you want to experience or perceived

____

____

____

I will manage ________________________ by purposefully recognizing when ______________ happens or is manifesting in negative behavior. To ensure success, I will ______________________ to clear or remove the chaos I am experiencing.

As a reminder, I will pay attention to the things below, to aid in my management of chaos.

What Negative Behavior Looks Like	What may Trigger the Negative Behavior	What action will mitigate Negative Behavior

Notes to Self

Activity 1: Working Through and Managing Chaos

What Chaos looks like ____

Is the Chaos ☐ External ☐ Internal ☐ Both

What caused the Chaos ☐ Self ☐ Work ☐ Family ☐ Political ☐ Religious

Other ____

The negative behavior (perception - what is seen or felt) of the chaos

____

____

____

Positive behavior you want to experience or perceived

____

____

____

I will manage ______________________ by purposefully recognizing when ______________ happens or is manifesting in negative behavior. To ensure success, I will ______________________ to clear or remove the chaos I am experiencing.

As a reminder, I will pay attention to the things below, to aid in my management of chaos.

What Negative Behavior Looks Like	What may Trigger the Negative Behavior	What action will mitigate Negative Behavior

Notes to Self

Activity 1: Working Through and Managing Chaos

What Chaos looks like ____

Is the Chaos ☐ External ☐ Internal ☐ Both

What caused the Chaos ☐ Self ☐ Work ☐ Family ☐ Political ☐ Religious

Other ____

The negative behavior (perception - what is seen or felt) of the chaos

____

____

____

Positive behavior you want to experience or perceived

____

____

____

I will manage ______________________ by purposefully recognizing when ______________ happens or is manifesting in negative behavior. To ensure success, I will ____________________ to clear or remove the chaos I am experiencing.

As a reminder, I will pay attention to the things below, to aid in my management of chaos.

What Negative Behavior Looks Like	What may Trigger the Negative Behavior	What action will mitigate Negative Behavior

Notes to Self

Activity 1: Working Through and Managing Chaos

What Chaos looks like ____

Is the Chaos ☐ External ☐ Internal ☐ Both

What caused the Chaos ☐ Self ☐ Work ☐ Family ☐ Political ☐ Religious

Other ____

The negative behavior (perception - what is seen or felt) of the chaos

____

____

____

Positive behavior you want to experience or perceived

____

____

____

I will manage ______________________ by purposefully recognizing when ______________ happens or is manifesting in negative behavior. To ensure success, I will ____________________ to clear or remove the chaos I am experiencing.

As a reminder, I will pay attention to the things below, to aid in my management of chaos.

What Negative Behavior Looks Like	What may Trigger the Negative Behavior	What action will mitigate Negative Behavior

Notes to Self

Activity 1: Working Through and Managing Chaos

What Chaos looks like ____

Is the Chaos ☐ External ☐ Internal ☐ Both

What caused the Chaos ☐ Self ☐ Work ☐ Family ☐ Political ☐ Religious

Other ____

The negative behavior (perception - what is seen or felt) of the chaos

____

____

____

Positive behavior you want to experience or perceived

____

____

____

I will manage ________________________ by purposefully recognizing when _______________ happens or is manifesting in negative behavior. To ensure success, I will ______________________ to clear or remove the chaos I am experiencing.

As a reminder, I will pay attention to the things below, to aid in my management of chaos.

What Negative Behavior Looks Like	What may Trigger the Negative Behavior	What action will mitigate Negative Behavior

Notes to Self

Workbook Appendix

Support Resources for Black Women Navigating Workplace Storms

"Healing isn't passive. It's power. Equip yourself with tools that affirm your worth, protect your peace, and guide your next move."

Emotional Health & Boundaries

Resource	Description	Use This When...
Set Boundaries, Find Peace by Nedra Glover Tawwab	A guide to asserting your limits with grace	You feel overwhelmed by others' demands
Therapy for Black Girls (Podcast)	Weekly tools for emotional healing and self-worth	You need a voice that "gets it"
Sacred Self-Care by Chanequa Walker-Barnes	Spiritually grounded care for women of color	You want to reconnect with your soul

My Go-To Boundary Phrase:

"I appreciate the ask, but I'm at capacity."

"I am not available for that right now."

Workbook Appendix

Leadership, Equity & Workplace Navigation

Resource	Description	Use This When...
The Memo by Minda Harts	Career strategies for women of color	You want to advocate for your next level
Lead From the Outside by Stacey Abrams	How to lead when you're not "let in"	You feel like the only one in the room
Lean In Workplace Reports	Data on equity, burnout, and leadership gaps	You want backup for speaking truth

Pro Tip: Bookmark: https://leanin.org/women-in-the-workplace

My Promotion Plan:

- My next move: ____
- My evidence of readiness: ________________________________
- Who supports me? _____________________________________

Workbook Appendix

Voices of Affirmation (Podcasts & Audio)

Podcast	Why It's Powerful
HerSpace with Terri Lomax & Dr. Dom	Healing from microaggressions, imposter syndrome, and burnout
Redefining Wealth with Patrice Washington	Reframes success beyond salary and title
Blessed + Bossed Up (Faith-based)	Helps you trust God's timing while building your legacy

My Affirmation Playlist Includes:

Workbook Appendix

Tools & Templates

Tool	Use It For
Burnout Self-Assessment	To recognize when you're slipping into survival mode
Boundary Scripts	Practice saying "no" without guilt
Life Raft Worksheet *(see Flooded section)*	Clarifying Support, Needs & Boundaries
Reset Statements *(Earthquake/Sinkhole sections)*	Mental/emotional boundaries when chaos hits

My Personal Reset Statement:

"I no longer ______________________________ to be seen."

"I honor my peace by ______________________________."

Workbook Appendix

Spiritual Grounding & Identity Restoration

Devotional/Tool	Why It Helps
Isaiah 43 Journal Prompt Series	Reaffirms God's presence in pressure
Be the Bridge (Latasha Morrison)	Combines faith and justice work
Our Bible App	Inclusive devotionals for healing identity wounds

Scriptures That Hold Me Steady:

Resources

Marie, J. (2024). Black Girls Breathing: Heal From Trauma, Combat Chronic Stress, and Find Your Freedom. Balance

Find Your Calm: Mindfulness cards to help you relieve anxiety and find mindfulness.

Made in the USA
Monee, IL
25 May 2026

50966365R00092